DATE DUE

DATE DUE			
JAN 3 1 2004			
GAYLORD			PRINTED IN U.S.A.

I want to be a Doctor

I WANT TO BE A

Doctor

DAN LIEBMAN

FIREFLY BOOKS

A Firefly Book

Published by Firefly Books Ltd. 2000

Copyright © 2000 Firefly Books Ltd.

First Printing 2000

U.S. Cataloging-in-Publication Data is available.

Canadian Cataloguing in Publication Data

Liebman, Daniel
    I want to be a doctor

ISBN 1-55209-463-4 (bound)   ISBN 1-55209-461-8 (pbk.)

1. Physicians – Juvenile literature. I. Title

R690.L53 2000   j610.69'52   C99-932467-5

Published in Canada in 2000 by
Firefly Books Ltd.
3680 Victoria Park Avenue
Willowdale, Ontario, Canada
M2H 3K1

Published in the United States in 2000 by
Firefly Books (U.S.) Inc.
P.O. Box 1338, Ellicott Station
Buffalo, New York, USA
14205

Photo Credits

© First Light/John Curtis, front cover.
© Schmid-Langsfeld, The Image Bank, page 5.
© Max Schneider, The Image Bank, page 6.
© Kay Chernush, The Image Bank, pages 7, 24.
© Weinberg/Clark, The Image Bank, pages 8-9.
© Juan Silva Productions, The Image Bank, back
    cover, pages 10, 21.
© Steve Niedorf Photography, The Image Bank,
    page 11.

© Jay Freis, The Image Bank, page 12.
© Alvis Upitis, The Image Bank, page 15.
© Ben Weaver, The Image Bank, page 16.
© Patti McConville, The Image Bank, page 17.
© Vladimir Lange, The Image Bank, page 18.
© Al Harvey, page 19.
© Kit Kittle/Corbis, page 20.
© Robert Graves/Corbis, page 21.
© Romilly Lockyer, The Image Bank, page 22.

Design by Interrobang Graphic Design Inc.
Printed and bound in Canada by Friesens, Altona, Manitoba

Canada

The Publisher acknowledges the financial support of the Government of Canada through the Book Publishing Industry Development Program for its publishing activities.

A strong light helps this doctor check the baby's ear.

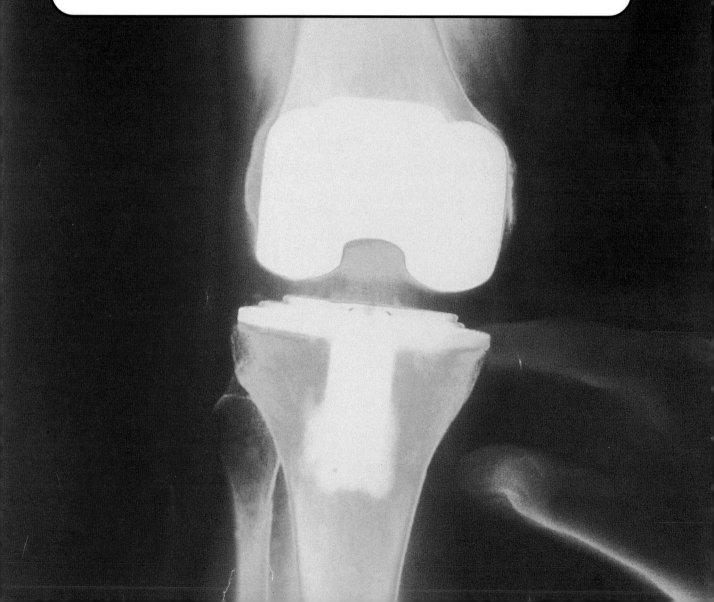

X-rays show doctors what your body looks like under the skin. The doctor is checking for broken bones.

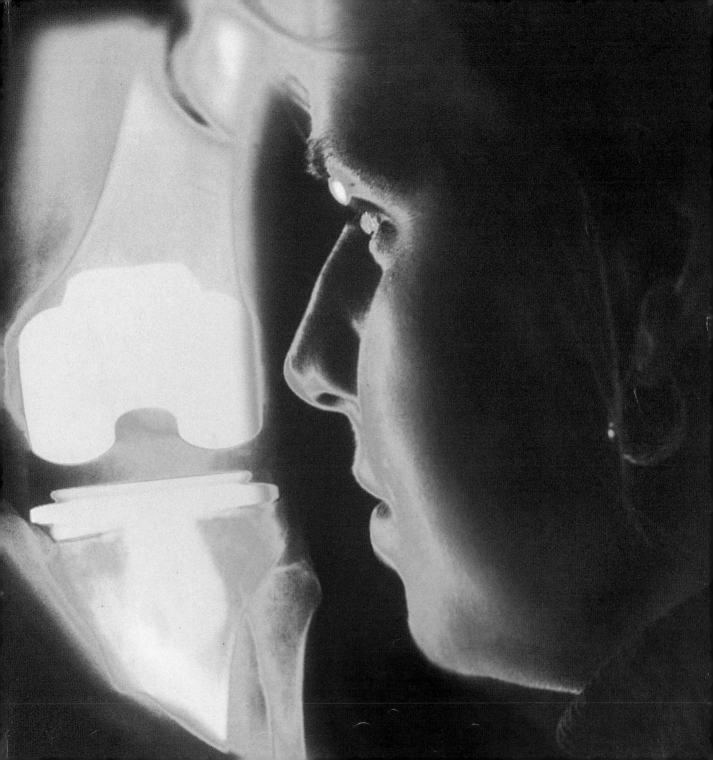

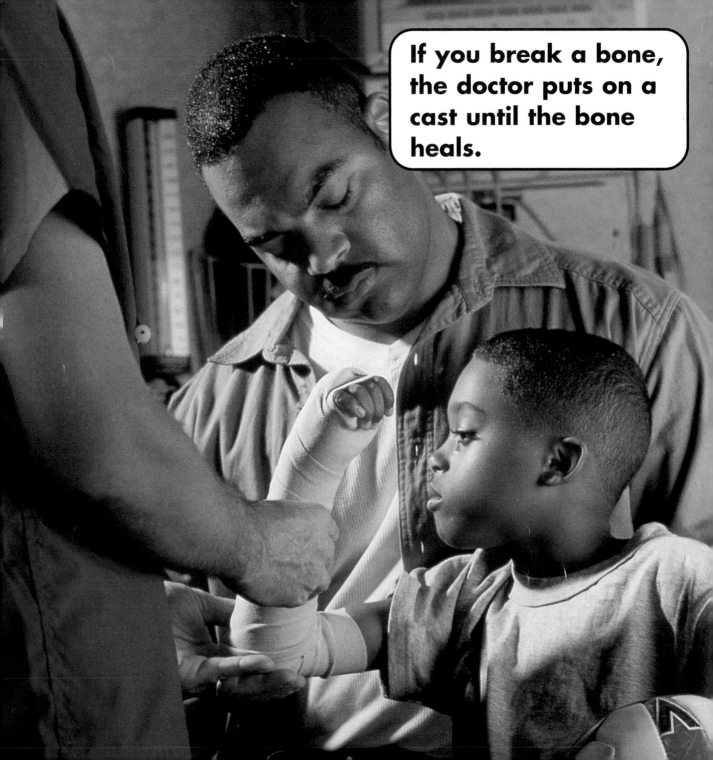

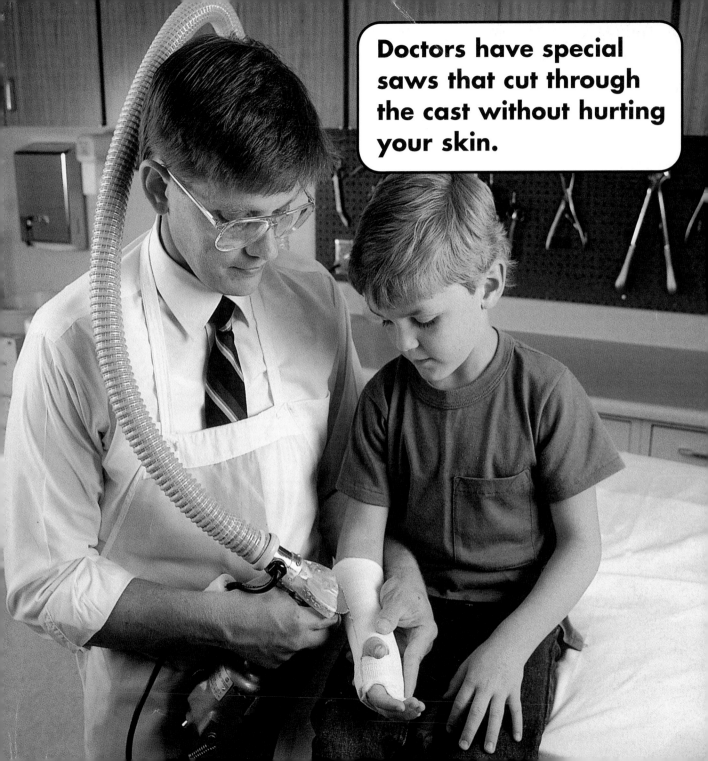

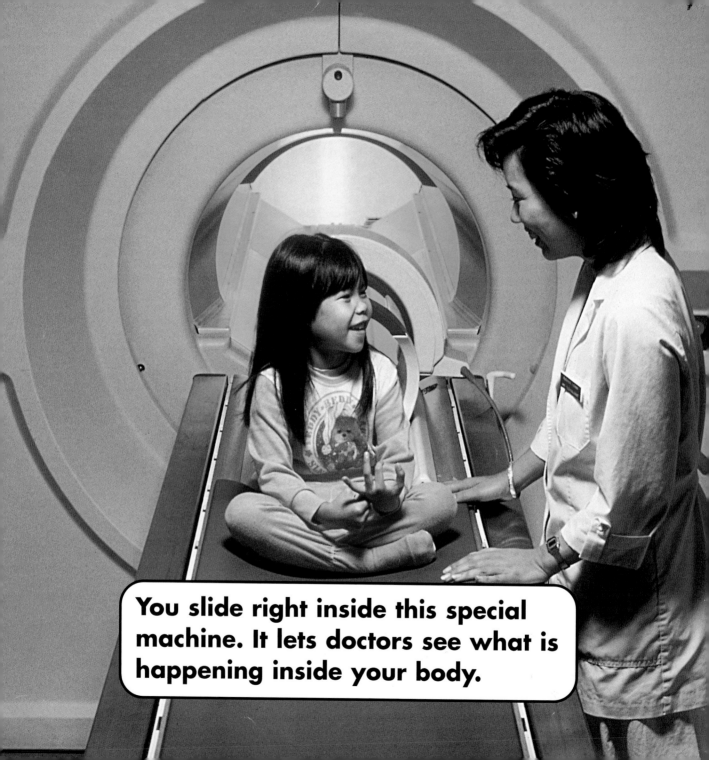

You slide right inside this special machine. It lets doctors see what is happening inside your body.

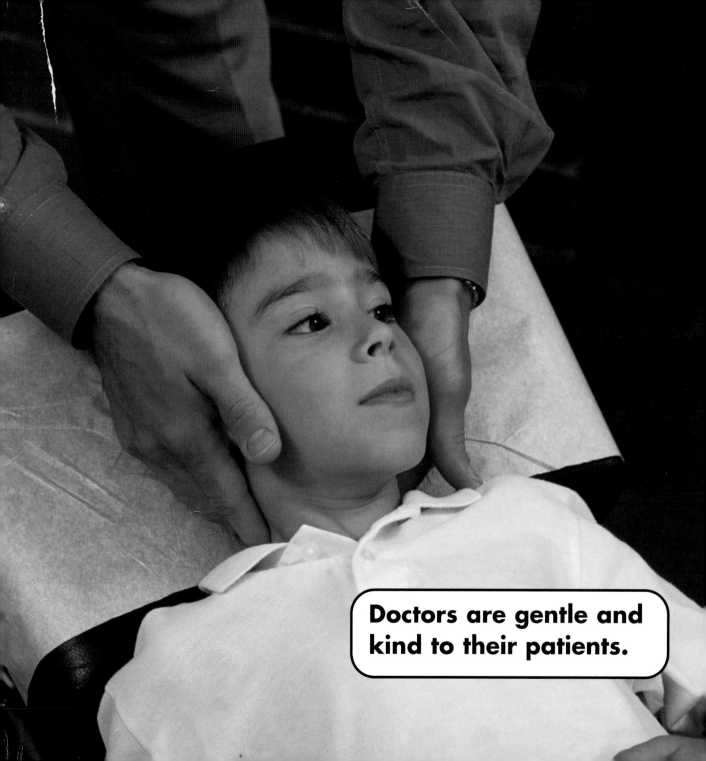

Doctors are gentle and kind to their patients.

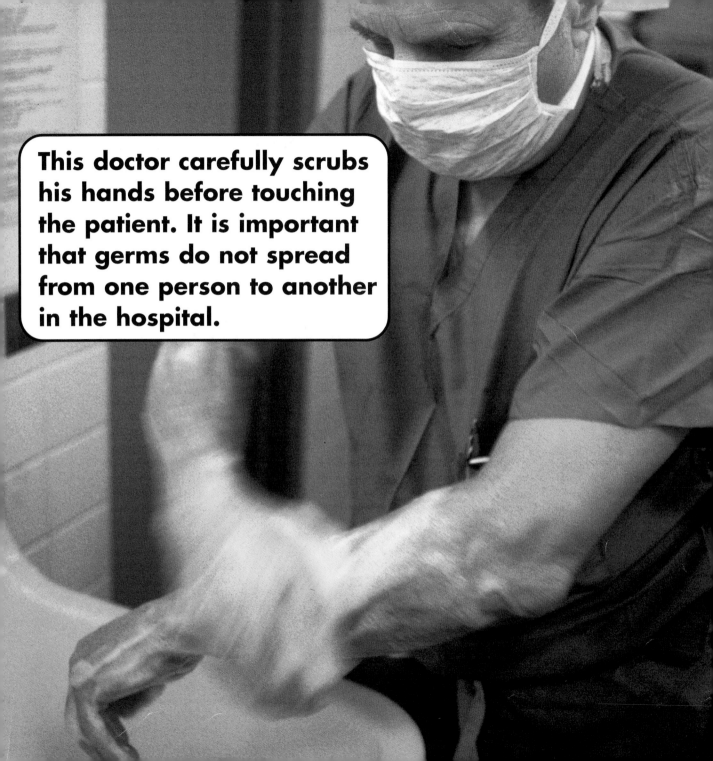

This doctor carefully scrubs his hands before touching the patient. It is important that germs do not spread from one person to another in the hospital.

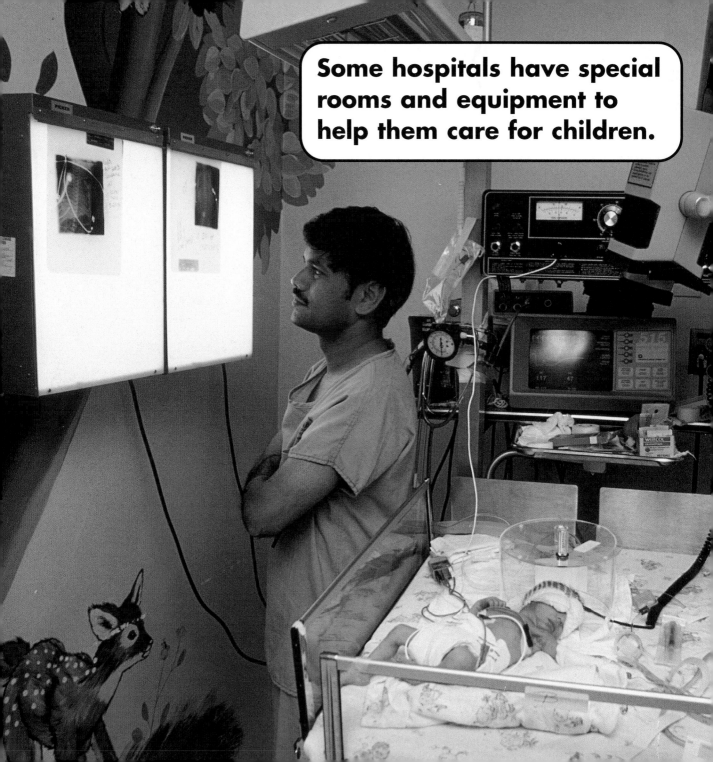

Some hospitals have special rooms and equipment to help them care for children.

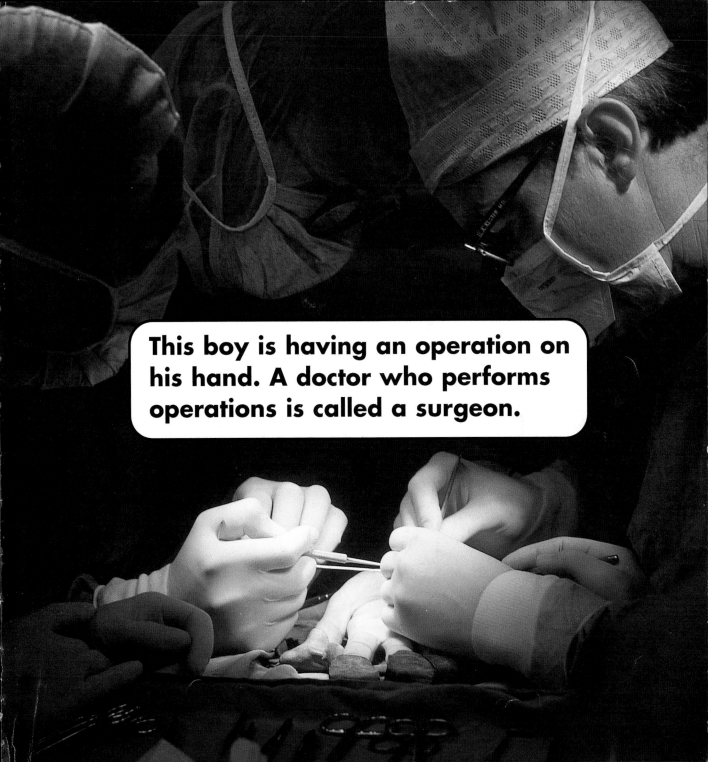

This nurse is showing the patient an x-ray while he is being flown to the hospital in an air ambulance.

Patients are strapped in carefully to prevent injury while flying.

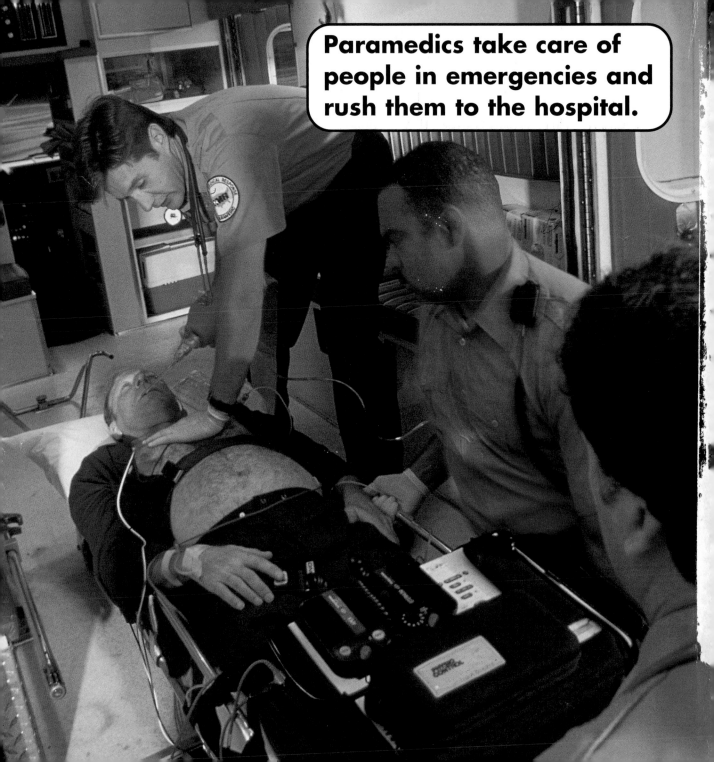

Paramedics take care of people in emergencies and rush them to the hospital.